Unusual and Awesome JOBS Using TECHNOLOGY

Roller Coaster Designer, Space Robotics Engineer, and More

by Linda LeBoutillier

CAPSTONE PRESS
a capstone imprint

Edge Books are published by Capstone Press,
1710 Roe Crest Drive, North Mankato, Minnesota 56003
www.capstonepub.com

Library of Congress Cataloging-in-Publication Data
LeBoutillier, Linda, author.
  Unusual and awesome jobs using technology : roller coaster designer, space robotics
engineer, and more / by Linda LeBoutillier.
    pages cm. -- (You get paid for THAT?)
  Includes bibliographical references.
  ISBN 978-1-4914-2029-4 (Hardcover)
  ISBN 978-1-4914-2200-7 (eBook PDF)
1. Technology--Vocational guidance--Juvenile literature. 2. Engineering--Vocational
guidance--Juvenile literature. 3. Occupations--Juvenile literature. I. Title.
  TA157.L42 2015
  602.3--dc23   2014040363

Editorial Credits
Editor: Nate LeBoutillier
Designer: Veronica Scott
Media researcher: Jo Miller
Production specialist: Tori Abraham

Photo Credits
Alamy: Greenshoots Communication/NCP Images, 29, Horizons WWP/Ton Koene, 11,
Ivan Nesterov, 15, Tony Watson, 13; Capstone Studio, 21; Corbis: BUCK Studio, 19; Getty
Images: National Geographic/Rodney Brindamour, 9; Newscom: UPI/BP, 26-27; Photoshot:
UPPA, 7; Robert Harding: David McLain, 25; Science Source: Brian Bell, 23, Science Photo
Library/James Stevenson, 17; Shutterstock: Alan Uster, cover (Earth), Doug Lemke, cover
(rollercoaster), Kun Kunko, cover (background), SIHASAKPRACHUM, 4-5

Printed in the United States of America in Stevens Point, Wisconsin.
092014   008479WZS15

TABLE OF CONTENTS

TICKLED BY TECHNOLOGY

If you're interested in learning about the latest gadgets, you'll love reading about the jobs in this book. Each job involves the use of state-of-the-art technology that allows people to do things easier, better, or more quickly than before.

And some of the technology allows workers to do jobs that used to be impossible! You already know about computers and digital cameras, but you may not have heard about Remotely Operated Vehicles (ROVs) for recovering sunken treasure, robots that work in space, or designers who create roller coasters. Soon you'll see that exciting careers abound in the world of technology.

ROLLER COASTER DESIGNER

Job Description: design roller coasters that are both fun and safe

Requirements: knowledge of physics and mechanical engineering

Technology Used: computer, CAD design software

Starting Salary: $24 per hour or around $50,000 per year

Top Salary: $119,400 per year

Hours: 40 hours a week, possible overtime

   Gravity constantly weighs on the mind of a roller coaster designer. Roller coaster designers know how gravity and the laws of motion work. Once a coaster has made it to the top of the first hill, gravity keeps it going all the way to the end of the ride. They use **physics** to calculate the top speed of the coaster and how big of a drop is necessary to make riders feel weightless as the coaster rushes down. Designers decide the height of the hills, the number of twists and turns, and the speed of the drops.

   Modern designers use Computer-Aided Design (CAD) or other software to design a track layout. This software automatically does hundreds of mathematical calculations that used to take months of work. Their goal is to make something that results in a thrilling—but safe—ride for passengers.

software—programs that make computers work

gravity—a force that pulls objects together; gravity pulls objects down toward the center of the Earth

physics—the science that deals with matter and energy

The Magnum XL-200 in Sandusky, Ohio

ANIMAL PSYCHOLOGIST

Job Description: measure intelligence in animals and teach them to communicate with humans

Requirements: advanced degree in psychology, experience with animals

Technology Used: computer, voice production software, voice synthesizer

Salary: $20,000 to $100,000 per year

Hours: normal full-time or part-time working hours

If chimps could talk, what would they say to humans? Animal psychologists at zoos and university labs teach chimps and orangutans to use human language. Technology plays an important part in this work.

Animals can't talk like humans do, so they use a voice **synthesizer**. It looks like a big-screen tablet with a touch screen and a special keyboard. Instead of letters, this keyboard uses symbols to stand for words the animal knows, such as "tree," "me," "good," "give," or "help."

The animals learn to touch symbols in the right order to make sentences. When the sentences are in order, the synthesizer reads the message in a human voice. As the animal learns new words, new picture symbols are programmed to appear.

synthesizer—a computer-controlled device that creates and modifies sound

YOU'D BETTER BELIEVE IT!

At Georgia State University, one chimp named Panbanisha had a vocabulary of 3,000 words. She could ask for iced coffee or talk about videos she watched using a special keyboard with 400 keys.

A scientist teaches sign language to an orangutan in Indonesia.

VIDEO GAME DESIGNER

HELP WANTED

Job Description: lead a team that designs and animates computer games

Requirements: knowledge of graphic design and animation

Technology Used: computer, handheld gaming device, graphics and animation software

Salary Range: $30,000 to $100,000 per year

Hours: normal full-time working hours

Imagine playing video games for a living. That's what game designers do, but they don't work alone. It's a team effort. Designers dream up the characters, settings, storylines, and rules for games. Then they work with graphic artists, **engineers**, writers, and **programmers** to produce the games. The designer keeps the team on track, often working on a tight deadline.

When a game is complete, the designer gets to play the game to see how it works. The designer fixes any problems before the game is sold in stores. The busiest time is autumn, because new games must be sent to stores in time for the holiday shopping season.

YOU'D BETTER BELIEVE IT!

The Disney Infinity Toy Box system uses characters from its Pixar movies. Using Toy Box, kids can create their own words or create games with their own rules.

engineer—a person who uses science, math, or technology to plan, design, or build

programmer—a person who creates computer programs

ROCK BAND SOUND ENGINEER

HELP WANTED

Job Description: oversee placement of equipment and balance the instruments and voices to make sure that the music sounds great

Requirements: knowledge of acoustics and electronics

Technology Used: microphones, amplifiers, audio lines, mixing board

Salary Range: $20,000 to $81,000 per year

Hours: anytime the band rehearses, records, or plays a gig

The audience is excited for the show to begin. Behind the curtain the musicians take their places. But long before the curtain goes up, the sound engineer has been hard at work setting up the stage and testing the equipment.

The **gig** might be in a concert hall, a nightclub, or a stadium. The band may be recording at a studio. Wherever the band is playing, the sound engineer is there making sure that each member of the band sounds right. **Acoustics** make music sound different in different places. The sound engineer makes sure all audience members can hear the music no matter how far away their seats are located.

gig—a live performance in front of an audience
acoustics—the qualities of a room or building that make it easy or hard to hear sounds

An engineer mixes sound at a Bon Jovi concert at Hyde Park in London in 2011.

Sound engineers work with microphones that pick up the sound. They work with audio cables that carry the sounds, and **amplifiers** that project the sound to the audience. They also work with monitors and **mixing boards**. With this equipment engineers can balance the instruments and voices to create a pleasing effect. Engineers must also know how to take care of equipment and what to do when there is an equipment problem. Sound engineers do whatever it takes to make sure that the musicians are pleased with their sound.

This job requires a willingness to work whenever the band needs them. Gigs or recording sessions can last for hours, far into the night. It may mean working evenings and weekends. It may mean traveling with a band in a tour bus for weeks on end.

Nightclub music in Amsterdam in 2014

YOU'D BETTER BELIEVE IT!

Geoff Emerick was the sound engineer for the Beatles, a famous rock band in the 1960s. Emerick started working for the Beatles at age 15. He could make a guitar sound like a trumpet by using the mixing board.

amplifier—a piece of equipment that makes sound louder

mixing board—a control panel for combining and adjusting musical sounds for a performance or recording

MEDICAL ILLUSTRATOR

Job Description: make drawings of surgical procedures in the operating room

Requirements: art talent and interest in health, science, or the medical field; master's degree in medical illustration

Technology Used: computer, graphics and animation software

Salary Range: $60,000 to $250,000 per year

Hours: flexible

HELP WANTED

The medical illustrator's job starts in the operating room. The illustrator's tools are not scalpels and clamps, but pencils, pens, and a sketchpad. The doctor explains what is happening, and the illustrator makes sketches showing each step of the surgery.

After the operation the illustrator scans drawings into a computer. Software helps add details that cannot be shown in a photo. **Illustrations** are colored and parts of the body are labeled. Some drawings are turned into digital images to be used in textbooks for health care workers. Some are turned into brochures about new medical devices for patients. Some drawings are turned into **animation** for videos.

Medical illustrators get to watch new surgical procedures and witness the first use of life-saving inventions. Their illustrations educate people about important advances in medicine.

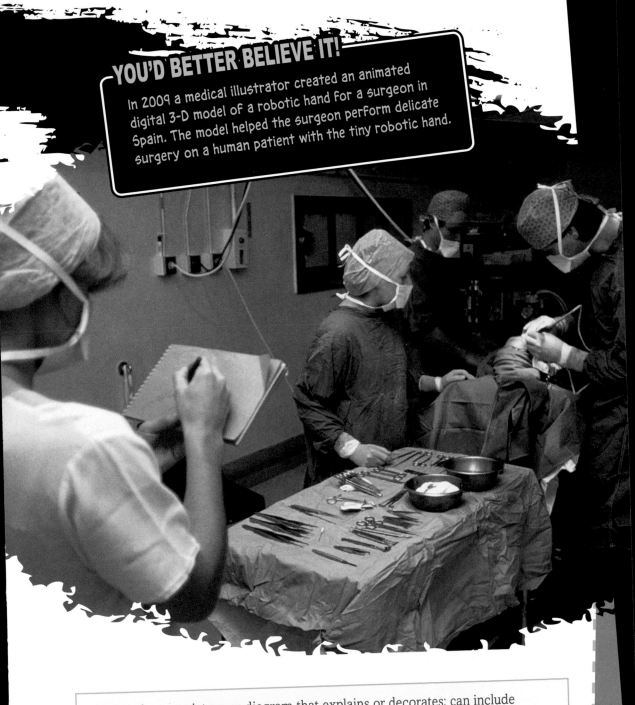

YOU'D BETTER BELIEVE IT!

In 2009 a medical illustrator created an animated digital 3-D model of a robotic hand for a surgeon in Spain. The model helped the surgeon perform delicate surgery on a human patient with the tiny robotic hand.

illustration—a picture or diagram that explains or decorates; can include drawings, photos, or digitally altered graphics

animation—a way of giving the appearance of movement to a series of drawings, graphics, or objects

17

SOFTWARE DEVELOPER

Job Description: design and develop software that makes almost any activity or process more convenient or efficient

Requirements: degree and experience in computer science and knowledge of math

Technology Used: computer, Internet programming software

Salary Range: $54,000 to $108,000 per year

Hours: regular full-time hours

HELP WANTED

The Internet changes fast. Software developers are the ones who make these changes happen. They have made it easier for us to search for information on the Internet. They have helped make it possible for us to use maps, shop, play games, and communicate with one another online. Who knows what they will think of next?

Software developers typically work on short-term projects lasting 6 to 12 months. They work in small teams that deliver results quickly. They enjoy solving problems and trying new things.

YOU'D BETTER BELIEVE IT!

Everything a computer does is based on ones and zeros that work like a light switch that can be turned on or off. Software designers understand how to turn ones and zeroes into usable information.

Software developers are constantly doing research to find new ways to serve people using the Internet. First, they decide what they want the computer to do based on people's needs. Then they use mathematical **algorithms** to program the steps for the computer to follow. Once they have designed a piece of software, they test it to make sure it works right every time. They work to fix any bugs in the program. Finally, they write instructions so that people can use the software successfully. They are often required to teach others to use the software for the first time.

People already work and shop from home. Someday they may be able to program their electric cars with directions to automatically take them to a family vacation spot. They may be able to order dinner in advance from any restaurant on the planet.

algorithm—a set of steps followed in precise order that are used to solve a problem or complete a computer process

PET PHOTOGRAPHER

Job Description: photograph pets in order to create representations of those photos, including prints, paintings, or graphic screens

Requirements: love of and ability to work safely around animals; knowledge of photography, graphic design, and computer software

Technology Used: high-end digital camera, computer, graphic arts software

Salary Range: $18,000 to $120,000 per year

Hours: 20-40 hours per week including seasonal work; higher demand from April through November; travel often required

People love keepsake photos and paintings of their pets. Unfortunately it's almost impossible to get animals to cooperate for a photo in just the right setting. Many photos of pets are altered somewhat in order to make them appear picture perfect. This is why top pet photographers use digital cameras and special computer software to enhance photos or turn them into **digital paintings**.

Pet photographers' cameras must have **zoom lenses** and other features that tell the camera exactly where to focus. Once photographers upload the photo proofs to a computer, the pet owner selects the desired photos. The photographer then **manipulates** the photos using a variety of techniques that can sharpen, fix, and recolor the photos. These are then made into different-sized prints or digital paintings. Some are screened onto items like coffee cups, calendars, or even T-shirts.

Photographer Karon gets to know her subject, a Mastiff named Smudge.

digital painting—an art object created with digital software on a computer

zoom lens—a lens on a camera in which the focal length can be continuously changed while the image remains in focus

manipulate—to change something by using editing techniques in order to create an illusion or deception after the original photographing took place

SPACE ROBOTICS ENGINEER

Job Description: design robots for space missions and communicate with these robots

Requirements: degree in computer science, mechanical engineering, or electrical engineering

Technology Used: computer, robots, design software, Internet networking software

Salary Range: $47,000 to $116,000 per year

Hours: normal full-time hours; overtime required during space missions

Space robotics engineers design equipment to be used in conditions unlike those on Earth. Space robots might work in the deep cold of outer space or the extreme heat of a planet such as Venus. They do their work in very low gravity.

Robotics engineers design and test robotic arms that make repairs on **space stations** or **satellites**. They create robots that can take pictures, study the soil, or look for the presence of life on a planet.

Engineers test robots under extreme conditions. They try to think of everything that could possibly go wrong. Once a robot is launched into space, it's too late to make most changes. However, some robots are programmed to make certain repairs themselves. Engineers can occasionally repair other robots by using remote control.

space station—a spacecraft that circles Earth in which astronauts can live for long periods of time

satellite—a spacecraft that circles Earth and gathers and sends information from one place to another

spacewalk—a task or mission performed by an astronaut in space outside of a spacecraft

ROV PILOT TECHNICIAN

Job Description: repair, maintain, launch, and operate ROVs; monitor and interpret data from the ROV

Requirements: degree in marine technology, environmental science and/or mechanical or electronic engineering

Technology used: ROV monitor and controls, cameras, computers, power tools, and electronic test equipment

Starting Salary: $300 per day, or $9,000 per rotation

Top Salary: $500 per day, or $15,000 per rotation

Hours: 12-hour shifts each day, 7 days a week, while at sea for a 30-day rotation; can work multiple rotations

The crew members watch nervously as the ROV slowly makes its way to the ocean's surface after retrieving an object from a sunken ship. Will it be valuable treasure or junk? Even if it's not gold or silver coins, the items could be of great historical value. ROV pilot technicians are some of the few who get to examine the treasure first.

YOU'D BETTER BELIEVE IT!

Treasure hunters can't always keep what they find. In 2007 Odyssey Marine Exploration found silver coins worth $500 million in a sunken Spanish ship. It was the richest treasure ever found. In 2012 a U.S. federal judge awarded the treasure to Spain.

remote—from a distance, without physical contact

Engineers direct an ROV 1,200 feet below the surface of the Black Sea.

Finding shipwrecks is difficult. But searchers can access historical records that give details about ships that sank. If a shipwreck that was carrying treasure is found, a ship with an ROV on board heads to the site. The pilot launches the ROV into the water and guides it to the wreck site. The pilot can operate the ROV from a control room on the ship. ROVs carry cameras and mechanical tools for cutting, grabbing, and lifting. The technician can switch tools underwater without bringing the ROV to the surface. With the ROV the technician can locate treasure, cut into a ship's hull, lift heavy objects out of the way, grab the treasure, and haul it to the surface.

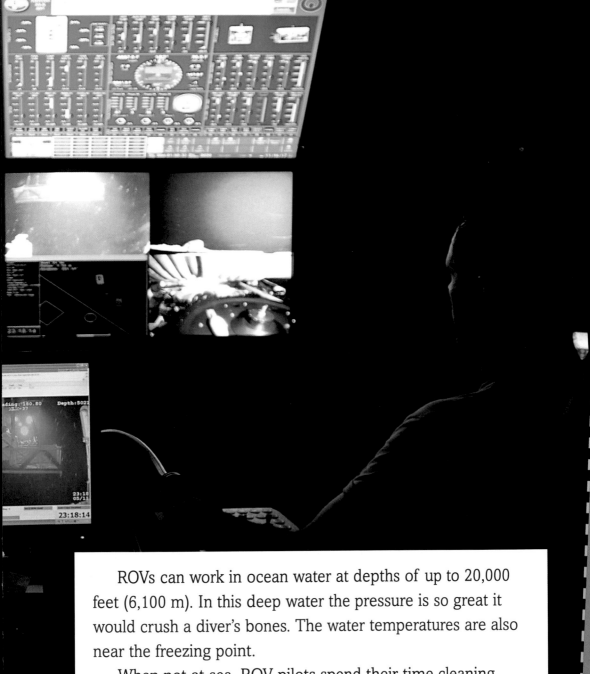

ROVs can work in ocean water at depths of up to 20,000 feet (6,100 m). In this deep water the pressure is so great it would crush a diver's bones. The water temperatures are also near the freezing point.

When not at sea, ROV pilots spend their time cleaning, repairing, and upgrading the ROVs. They must be able to use hand and power tools as well as advanced computers and high-definition (HD) camera equipment.

WIND TURBINE TECHNICIAN

HELP WANTED

Most jobs involving technology aren't very physically demanding. The job of a wind **turbine** technician is an exception. The work is done outdoors, often in harsh weather. Wind turbines are built in places where the wind is strong and steady. In the United States these places include the deserts of the Southwest, the plains of the Midwest, and the tundra in the North.

Wind technicians help with construction of new towers and maintenance of existing towers. Construction is seasonal, but maintenance continues all year. Technicians climb up the tower to work in the **nacelle**, where the computer controls and engine are located. They check and clean the motor and gearbox and grease-moving parts. They reset **sensors** and replace warning lights. In winter they remove ice from the turbine's turning blades.

YOU'D BETTER BELIEVE IT!

In 2013 there were wind installations in 39 states and Puerto Rico. The top five states for wind power capacity were Texas, California, Iowa, Illinois, and Oregon.

turbine—an engine powered by steam or gas; the steam or gas moves through the blades of a fanlike device and makes it turn

nacelle—a streamlined housing area located at the top of a wind turbine tower

sensor—a device that measures temperature, wind speed, and other physical properties

GLOSSARY

acoustics (uh-KOO-stiks)—the qualities of a room or building that make it easy or hard to hear sounds

algorithm (AL-guh-rith-uhm)—a set of steps followed in precise order that are used to solve a problem or complete a computer process

amplifier (AM-pluh-fy-uhr)—a piece of equipment that makes sound louder

animation (a-nuh-MAY-shuhn)—a way of giving the appearance of movement to a series of drawings, graphics, or objects

digital painting (DI-juh-tuhl PAYN-ting)—an art object created with digital software on a computer

engineer (en-juh-NEER)—a person who uses science, math, or technology to plan, design, or build

gig (GIG)—a live performance in front of an audience

gravity (GRAV-uh-tee)—a force that pulls objects together; gravity pulls objects down toward the center of the Earth

illustration (il-uh-STRAY-shuhn)— a picture or diagram that explains or decorates; can include drawings, photos, or digitally altered graphics

manipulate (muh-NIP-yuh-late)—to change something by using editing techniques in order to create an illusion or deception after the original photographing took place

mixing board (MIX-ing BORD)—a control panel for combining and adjusting musical sounds for a performance or recording

nacelle (nuh-SEL)—a streamlined housing area located at the top of a wind turbine tower

physics (FIZ-iks)—the science that deals with matter and energy

programmer (PRO-gram-er)—a person who creates computer programs

remote (ri-MOHT)—from a distance, without physical contact

satellite (SAT-uh-lite)—a spacecraft that circles Earth and gathers and sends information from one place to another

sensor (SEN-sur)—a device that measures temperature, wind speed, and other physical properties

software (SAWFT-wayr)—programs that make computers work

space station (SPAYSS STAY-shuhn)—a spacecraft that circles Earth in which astronauts can live for long periods of time

spacewalk (SPAYSS-wahk)—a task or mission performed by an astronaut in space outside of a spacecraft

synthesizer (SIN-thuh-sye-zur)—a computer-controlled device that creates and modifies sound

turbine (TUR-bine)—an engine powered by steam or gas; the steam or gas moves through the blades of a fanlike device and makes it turn

zoom lens (ZOOM LENS)—a lens on a camera in which the focal length can be continuously changed while the image remains in focus

READ MORE

Graham, Ian. *Technology Careers*. In the Workplace. Mankato, Minn.: Amicus, 2011.

La Bella, Laura. *Careers in Web Development*. Careers in Computer Technology. New York: Rosen Publishing, 2011.

INTERNET SITES

FactHound offers a safe, fun way to find Internet sites related to this book. All of the sites on FactHound have been researched by our staff.

Here's all you do:

Visit *www.facthound.com*

Type in this code: 9781491420294

CRITICAL THINKING USING THE COMMON CORE

1. Think about the ways humans have interacted with animals through the ages. Look at the picture on page 9. In what ways do people treat animals differently today than they used to 50, 100, or 500 years ago? (Integration of Knowledge and Ideas)

2. The text on page 28 discusses the job of wind turbine technician. Using wind for energy is a relatively new idea. Can you think of other ways that humans may harness natural resources to bring about more efficient energy than by using fossil fuels such as oil and coal? (Craft and Structure)

INDEX